I0434907

WORDS TO WRITE BY
PUTTING YOUR THOUGHTS ON PAPER

ELAINE L. ORR

WORDS TO WRITE BY
PUTTING YOUR THOUGHTS ON PAPER

Elaine L. Orr

Create Space Edition

Copyright 2015 Elaine L. Orr

All rights reserved. Except for brief passages quoted in a review, no part of this book may be reproduced or transmitted in any form or by any means, electronic or mechanical, including photocopying, recording or by any information storage and retrieval system, without permission in writing from the author.

elaineorr55@yahoo.com.

www.elaineorr.com

http://www.elaineorr.blogspot.com

Copyright © 2015 Elaine L. Orr

ISBN-13: 978-1506166124
ISBN-10: 1506166121

TABLE OF CONTENTS

PREFACE
WHY READ THIS BOOK?

CHAPTER ONE   1
WHY AND WHO

CHAPTER TWO   5
PLANNING YOUR WRITING

CHAPTER THREE   11
THE FIRST DRAFT: SUBSTANCE OVER FORM

CHAPTER FOUR   14
CLEAR WRITING MAKES READING EASIER

CHAPTER FIVE   21
TAKING THE FEAR OUT OF REVISING YOUR WORK

CHAPTER SIX   23
WHERE DO YOU GO FROM HERE?

AUTHOR BIO   25

MORE BOOKS   25

WORK SHEETS   27

PREFACE
WHY READ THIS BOOK?

If you can talk, you can write. You can also read a lot of very long books about writing, and most of them are pretty good. I have read some of them. As a professional editor, I have also read some very poor writing. The difference between good writers and mediocre ones is whether they organize their thoughts before they put pens to paper.

Writing is a learned skill, not something that you either can or cannot do. The distinction between people who seem to write easily and those who do not is more a matter of comfort, exposure, and just plain doing it. If your parents and early teachers played word games with you or encouraged you to read, you may be more at ease with language in spoken and written form. If you didn't have early exposure, you can create greater comfort with words for yourself.

This book will deal with writing non-fiction, though the concept of developing your thoughts well applies to a short story or novel. Do you have an idea for an article? Has your boss said you need to learn to write better? Do you want to write your family history? Learn, at your own pace, how to put your thoughts on paper in a way that encourages others to read them.

Read on.

CHAPTER ONE
WHAT AND WHO?
THE APPROACH TO THIS BOOK

There are two key points for adults who want to learn to write well.

1. Don't be afraid to write badly while you learn.
2. Practice by writing about what you know.

In school, you had to learn about a subject before you began to write (such as term papers in high school), and your grade depended on how well you learned it and expressed what you knew. In this book, you will be encouraged to write about topics with which you are already familiar. Thus, you will not struggle with unfamiliar facts or ideas. You can focus on how to put these ideas on paper.

Pick a subject and think about it as you read this book, and use that subject to do the suggested exercises. If a subject does not come immediately to mind think about what you like to
- Read about
- Talk about
- Play

Play? Yes, play. Do you like to play basketball or Yahtzee? Maybe the topic you pick will have to do with strategies for winning a game. Perhaps you enjoy giving gifts and work hard to select them. The important thing is to pick something you like and know a lot about. If it seems like a trivial topic – no problem. Be assured, there is no topic so mundane that someone has not written about it. Why not you?

If you are reading this under the pressure of a deadline ("I have to finish the memo by tomorrow afternoon"), it will still benefit you to take a step back and write about what you know as you work through the practice sessions in this book.

DIFFERENT KINDS OF WRITING

To illustrate some of the different kinds of writing, think about plumbing. What kinds of pieces might you write about plumbing?
- Teaching manual for master plumbers
- Homeowner's guide for self-repair
- Humorous piece about why you don't do your own plumbing repairs anymore

There are many other kinds of writing, but the point is that any of these pieces could talk about fixing a pipe or installing a garbage disposal. Your vocabulary and tone will vary depending on why you are writing it and who you expect to read it.

Think About Your Goals

Sometimes the purpose of your writing is very clear – you need to communicate directly with the company vice-president to explain why it is difficult to work in an office with a leaking roof. You can do that via a memo, email, or letter, but the basic product will be a brief office communication. Other times, there is something you want to say, but you are not sure of the form you want to use to express the idea.

Consider some of the different kinds of writing.

Information or expository writing is designed to instruct the reader. Such writing would be in a news article, textbook, or encyclopedia, and can be heard as radio newscasts. It does not need to be in such a formal publication. You'll see expository writing in a church newsletter or city tour guide. (Instructions included with VCRs are not good examples of expository writing, as the author has never been able to figure out how to program any of hers. This example tells you how long ago the first draft of this book was written.)

Feature writing is designed to tell a story, but in a lighter form than a news article. It includes the articles in the magazine that comes with your Sunday newspaper, as well as many of those in magazines such as *Sports Illustrated* or *People*. Magazines such as *Time* or *Newsweek* have a mix of expository, feature, and editorial writing.

Essays put forth what you think about something, and have gained great popularity recently. Perhaps as baby boomers age they want to share their perspectives. You can read books of essays by famous people, but the most general examples of essays are newspaper columns or guest editorials. Two particularly good writers (at the opposite ends of the political spectrum) are Ellen Goodman and George Will. Neither writes as regularly now, but you can search for their work online. They are often reprinted. An essay does not have to be conveyed in writing. National Public Radio (NPR) features a number of essays every day, and not all of them are written and read by famous people, either.

Memoirs are reflective, but more personal than most essays. Anyone can write their memoirs; though children and grandchildren may tire of repeated stories, they often appreciate having family elders write short stories of their lives. Nearly every president has written memoirs. My favorite memoirs are Rose Kennedy's *Times to Remember* and Frank McCourt's *Angela's Ashes*.

Family histories can also be reflective, but are usually more concerned with presenting genealogical information than personal stories. Good organization is important. The writer is very familiar with the subject, but new people may continue to read a family history for literally dozens or hundreds of years. The better family histories separate facts from stories, and never refer to people as "my father's mother" or Great Uncle Hugo.

Business writing takes many forms and requires more precision than most other forms. It includes but is not limited to:

- Memos, letters, and email
- Reports
- Your employees' performance appraisals
- Press releases
- Policy manuals
- Company newsletters or magazines
- Reports

Humor. It's hard to describe, but you know it when you see it. Though columnists such as Dave Barry may come to mind first, people earn a living writing funny birthday cards and the jokes that comedians use. (The exception is those who write the jokes that get passed around on the Internet. No payment for them, usually for good reason!)

You can think of many other kinds of writing – training guides, advertising copy, or video game stories.

There are three components every kind of writing has in common – a beginning, a middle, and an end. When writing is poorly organized, it is hard for the reader to tell the beginning from the middle. They always know the end; you have to hope they have not been praying for it.

WHO WILL READ WHAT YOU WRITE?

In real estate, the three most important keys to a sale are said to be location, location, location. With your writing, what you say is important, but the key is audience, audience, audience. If you are writing about plumbing repairs, your style will be vastly different if your book is for plumbers taking a refresher course for license renewal or the new homeowner who does not know one end of a wrench from another.

Will everyone who reads your piece know pretty much the same thing about the topic? For example, if you are a soccer coach writing your welcome letter for the ten-year old players' parents (in which you exhort them not to throw things at you during a game), will most parents know a lot about the game, or will the only soccer vocabulary some know be the word "ball?"

Are you appealing to a certain age group? If you are writing about the need to plan for your retirement while young, your target audience is probably 25 to 35. In addition to different financial information than you might provide for a 50-year old, your examples of spending habits would differ. You don't want to refer to the tradeoffs between saving and taking a cruise, you would probably refer to saving versus buying expensive exercise equipment.

Are you writing to inform or persuade the reader? If you want to persuade, you will present information and then urge the reader to form a certain opinion based on it. If your piece is strictly an informational one, the reader does not need to know your opinion at all.

Are you writing just for your own benefit? If that is the case (as in writing in a journal) your vocabulary, tone, and structure are totally at your discretion. If you are reading this book, you probably want someone else to read what you write, so you need to continue to think audience, audience, audience.

If you are writing for work or a local newspaper, check to see if there is someone who defines the audience. For example, if you are writing for the union newsletter, it may be read by a lot of people, but the target audience is the union member. The editor will want every article to be written with the members in mind, not management. You may approach the article differently if you know this.

CHAPTER TWO
PLANNING YOUR WRITING
THE JUMBLE OF IDEAS IS A GOOD THING

The word *outline* conjures memories of strict English teachers and word processing software that doesn't let you indent the way you want and keeps putting in a lowercase "a" when you want an uppercase "A." Because of these negative connotations, you may want to think of a synonym, such as the framework of your ideas or the building blocks for your writing. What you are doing is planning what you will write.

THE IDEA PYRAMID

At the bottom: Jumble of Ideas
Midway: Grouping Like Ideas Together
At the top: Clear Sense of Direction

1. Decide on your audience

Everything else flows from this, whether you are writing fiction or nonfiction. Go no further until it is very clear who you want to read what you are planning to write.

2. Decide on your purpose

This may seem very clear as you start, but it may not be as clear as you think. Remember that plumbing repair work discussed previously? Suppose the roof in your office leaks during a heavy rain. The primary purpose of the memo to your boss could be to: authorize contacting a plumber immediately; suggest moving you to a different office; put in a pitch for new carpet after the plumber finishes the repair; rub in the point that you mentioned the small water spot months ago, and if the boss had acted then there would not be a geyser in your office. (The latter is not recommended.)

3. Decide on the tone and person.

You usually know the kind of product you have to write (newsletter article, memo to the boss). You also need to decide whether you will use formal or informal language and what person you will use.

<u>First person</u>: uses the words I and we. Use first person when your opinion is a focal point (an editorial).

<u>Second person</u>: uses the word you. This is a more conversational style.

<u>Third person</u>: a less personal style of writing. If a pronoun is necessary, it would be he, she or (more formally) "one." Newspaper and much business writing is done in the third person.

You can mix first and third person and first and second, but it is rare to see all three used in one piece. For example, if you are writing an opinion piece (such as a letter to the editor or a memo to your boss), you may write a good deal of it in third person, as you present information. At some point, you may also give your own opinion.

4. Make a list.

There may be twenty things you want to say. You have no idea of the order for presentation and the ideas may seem like a jumble at this point. Write it all down. Don't think about order, level of importance, or whether something is a fact or a conclusion you have drawn from some facts.

This list may not be complete until you finish your article or memo, because new ideas may come to you. That's fine. You need a starting point, and it does not have to look pretty.

5. Organize your ideas.

Study your list. If it is short, you may be able to mentally group similar ideas together. Generally, you will look for common themes or related information. Write each of these common themes on a different page or across the top of a single page, and then put similar topics in the same column or on the same page. Obviously, you can do this on your computer, too.

Use these groupings of topics to help you narrow your focus whenever you can. You only want to deal with what you have to deal with to make your point. That may seem obvious, but if you do not consciously eliminate unnecessary segments you will spend too much time writing and then have to edit out the extra verbiage.

6. Decide what comes first.

The key for deciding what to say first is to determine what your readers need to know before they can continue reading. What are some factors to consider in deciding on the order?

- Do you need to state the purpose of the piece at the beginning? This is common in memo and report writing.
- Does the material need to be in chronological order? That might be important if you were writing a vendor to explain what went wrong in the ordering and shipping process. It may not matter at all if you are writing a performance appraisal.
- Will your reader understand why something is important if they don't have background information? If they won't, put that first.
- Should the most important piece of information go first, or should you lead up to that? This is a judgment call. If you are writing for a busy reader, it may make sense to put the most important information first, just as a good newspaper article would.

7. Think about how the piece will end.

You will not know when you have finished writing if you don't know what constitutes "being done." The ending may be a two-sentence summary of the entire piece. Other times it will be the persuasive paragraph that encourages a reader to change a behavior or act on your recommendation.

8. Talk to someone about the idea.

Once you have a well-formulated idea (which this outline or listing process should help you achieve), consider talking to someone about it. This may not always be necessary or appropriate, but the more complex the piece the more you might benefit from seeking input from others.

9. Act as if you are working in pencil.

No list is finite, no idea is unchangeable. You may write with a pen, but don't hesitate to add or subtract from your list, or even redefine the purpose of your piece.

10. Collect your facts.

This is not really part of the idea development process, but you can't go from your list or outline to writing until you have all (or most) of the information you need. You don't want to spend so much time gathering information that you have to rush the writing, but you also don't want to be jumping up every five minutes to look up facts and figures.

What's Next?

It will give more meaning to the idea development process if there is an example rather than just a generic discussion. As of now, you have been commissioned to write a feature article for the weekly community newspaper on "How to Plan a Family Reunion." Good Luck.

FIRST CUT AT THE IDEA LIST

This is a free-flowing list. Don't try to edit as you write.

Family Reunion Ideas
Find good place
Indoors or outdoors?
Contacting everyone
Charge money so no one gets stuck with bills
How to avoid inviting someone
Include children or adults only?
Time of year to hold it
Need a plan to clean up trash
No pets
Planning ahead

Committee to plan so no one gets all the blame
Beer and wine only. No way. No booze
Bring pictures

As you can see, there is no order to this list. The writer scribbled whatever came to mind. If you read the list, you can think of things to add, and you are not even writing the article. The writer will continue to add to it.

Next, the author groups ideas into a Refined Idea List, shown below. Though this list is presented in outline form, there is no reason you have to use this format. The important thing is to find a way of grouping like ideas together, and to begin to think of the sequence in which you would present them.

At the beginning of the list, the writer has made notes to herself about the broad purposes of the article and how she wants to start.

REFINING THE IDEA LIST

General paragraph on why reunions are fun, but planning is the key. Note this article will deal with reunions that involve people coming from many locations.

A. Starting the planning process
- Start at least six months in advance
- Get people from all branches of the family on a planning committee
- Use email if you can, but snail mail probably needed for older family members

B. Developing the list of people to invite
- Key to the process – people will be hurt if you miss them
- Get current addresses informally and on the Internet
- Put the address list on the computer so there can be multiple sets of labels
- Decide how many notices to send and who will send them
- Discuss if young children should be included
- Emphasize no pets, please

C. Picking the location
- Discuss how to pick a central location
- Important that the location be near airports or rail stations
- Location will affect cost – church basement vs. restaurant

D. Planning some entertainment
[Note this is not on the original idea list.]
- Encourage everyone to bring pictures to share
- If you don't plan something, people will improvise

E. What to do about food
- Catered is more expensive
- Food-borne illnesses a risk if people bring food
- No alcohol, so driving home is not an issue

F. Day of the event

- Have name tags
- Keep your sense of humor
- Ask for volunteers to help pick up trash or lock doors

G. Closing out the day

- Pass a donation plate if necessary
- Ask people to send their address changes to a central location
- Announce the date of the next reunion and ask for volunteers

This refined list is grouped by ideas and has a number of points that were not on the original list. As the writer worked, she thought of details she had overlooked initially. The writer also left out one of the items on the initial list – how to avoid inviting someone. She decided that this would be too difficult to address.

GETTING TO WORK

NOW IT'S YOUR TURN

At the beginning of this book, it suggests that you select something you know and practice your writing with this familiar topic. If you still cannot think of something, think of what you would most rather do when you have house guests you don't like. You would rather play golf when the in-laws visit? Write about golf.

Writing about what you know is essential for this exercise. If you do your first practice session with a work project it could impede your ability to think freely and focus on the writing process. Your goal may be to write smooth products at the office, but leave the office out of your first effort.

You can photocopy the two workbook pages at the end of this book (and only those pages), and use them for other writing projects. Put on your thinking cap and let the ideas flow.

CREATING THE INITIAL IDEA LIST
- Who will read this?
- What kind of writing is this (memo, essay article, etc.)?
- What is your primary purpose in writing this?
- Off the top of your head, what are some of the topics you will discuss?

1.

2.

3.

4.

5. Keep Going with ideas. There are works sheets at the end of the book.

6.

7.

8.

9.

10.

REFINING YOUR IDEA LIST

     Take a short break, so you get some distance from your initial ideas.

     Reread your list. See if some of the ideas are linked to other ideas.

     Write down the two or three (or four or five) major themes on your list.

1.

2.

3.

4.

5. Use the work sheet at the end for more space.

     There are lots of other questions to ask yourself.

- Are some of these items more important than others? If so, list them.
- If you say only one thing about your topic, what would it be?
- Will this be the main point in your piece, or should it be?
- Do you want to lead with your main point, or do you want to present information that builds up to that point before you present it?
- How do you plan to end your piece? If you are not sure, jot a couple ideas and come back to this.
- Do you need to gather any information about your ideas before you start to write? If so, list what you need or some places to look. (Remember, don't get bogged down here.)

     Put these responses aside for a while (preferably overnight). Then reread them and make changes if you need to do so.

TURNING THE REFINED LIST INTO AN OUTLINE

     After you have given your Refined Idea List a little quiet time, reread it and start to think about what part of your piece you will begin with, and the order for the rest of it. The answers to the questions on your Refined Idea List should help you do this.

     If you cannot decide on the order for your outline, then group the like ideas together and think of these groupings as interchangeable building blocks.

     You may even find it useful to cut up the paper with the groupings of ideas and then put them in the order you think you want them for your piece. If that doesn't look right, move them around until you are comfortable enough to start writing.

     The pieces will fit together.

CHAPTER THREE
THE FIRST DRAFT
SUBSTANCE OVER FORM

As you start to move from your list or outline to writing paragraphs, you may feel a cold sweat coming on. Grab a sweater. No one has to read the first draft but you. You will appreciate the time you spent developing your ideas into an outline or list. Follow it, but don't be afraid to reorder or drop segments. Don't worry about spelling or grammar just yet. They come later.

If you are writing a three-chapter report, every chapter has a beginning, middle and end. If you are writing a one-page letter-to-the editor about the upcoming school board election, you will have the same three segments.

Because there cannot be a section of this book on all types of writing, this chapter will continue to discuss the Refined Idea List for the article on "How to Plan the Family Reunion."

THE OPENING PARAGRAPH
AND EARLY SECTIONS

Your piece has to establish its purpose in its introductory paragraph(s). In this article for the local newspaper, you want to grab the reader's attention, so you stress that they can have a good time, but only if they plan well for the reunion day. You are making an implicit promise that this article will help them create and experience a good reunion.

The reunion article talks about planning as a process (in Section A) and then addresses what to plan (Sections B through D). Thus, the first few paragraphs will deal with the importance of planning and give an overview of the process.

The paragraph is the mechanism for grouping sentences together so the piece deals with similar topics in the same part of the article. If you are writing a report, it may be divided into major sections, but within those sections the paragraphs should each contain a well-developed idea. Paragraphs may introduce a new point, or may continue building an existing idea.

THE BODY OF THE ARTICLE

Unless you are writing a brief memo or short announcement, there are generally a number of topics with which to deal. In developing your Refined Idea List, you created topic groupings, and these become the basis for the sections of your article.

It can be hard to transition from one idea to the next. If you are writing a newspaper article or report, you have the advantage of subtitles (as in this book), and they announce the new topic. For the family reunion article, the Refined Idea List groups the topics by what the planners have to do first, then leads into the event itself. If you have trouble with transitions, write about each topic, and then read what you have written from the perspective of how they flow together. For example, as you end the section about the location, you might mention that some locations lend themselves to one kind of entertainment rather than another. Voila. You're talking about whether to have banjos or Brahms.

Not every topic requires the same length of discussion. For example, entertainment might be worthy of only one paragraph, but you may have so much to say about whom to invite that this becomes three paragraphs. Still, you want to keep like ideas together. Talk about finding people just once, not at the beginning and end of the section on inviting family.

Try to avoid telling the reader what you are doing; just do it. For example, there is no need to say, "The next section will talk about how to develop the list of people to invite." Simply say, "There is no point in having a reunion if you don't invite as many people as possible."

If you are writing a persuasive piece (remember that new carpet you wanted for your office because of the leaky ceiling?), you will provide information in the body that supports your final conclusion – you need the carpet. You could discuss the age of the carpet, mention that it is hard to thoroughly clean mildew, or cite the fact that there is excess money in the company budget, which would make the purchase possible.

In the family reunion article, it could get to sound like a lecture if you just tell readers what they "should" do. The writer may throw in some examples from reunions she has attended. Remember how Uncle Timothy sang fourteen Irish ballads at the last reunion? That's why you plan entertainment; no one wants to sit through something like that. (That could also serve as one of the examples for why there is no alcohol.)

GETTING TO THE END

This is the hardest part for some people. How do you know when to stop? Sometimes you have a prescribed length, but even then, what do you pick for the last paragraph or sentence?

The family reunion article chose to make the end of this year's reunion be the planning process for the next one. That goes with the overall theme that planning is essential. It could just as easily have ended with a couple of the planners reflecting on what a good time they had. Endings are a choice.

Don't worry about the exact wording for your ending. Make sure you have made all your points. If your piece is a persuasive one, your ending will suggest what you think the readers should do – buy the carpet, vote for Abraham Lincoln. If your piece is informational, you may end with the most or least important piece of information (depending on how you structured the article). You may choose to summarize the most important two pieces of information.

Stop writing when you are comfortable, and put away the article to read later. It would be helpful if you can wait until the next day, but if you can't, walk down the hall or get a drink of water – something to help you get some distance from what you just wrote.

CHAPTER FOUR
CLEAR WRITING MAKES READING EASIER

Although you can avoid paying much attention to grammar and spelling in your first draft, ultimately you have to have what an editor calls "clean copy." Besides, if you are going to the trouble of writing something, you want your readers to understand it easily. This chapter discusses good habits for clear writing as well as some common grammar and punctuation problems. You will want to keep these things in mind as you revise your first draft, which is what you will deal with in Chapter Five.

CLEAR WRITING

Two keys to writing clearly are using a straightforward vocabulary and using active voice instead of passive voice. You don't need to worry about these choices so much in your first draft, but as you become more familiar with clear writing habits your first draft will get easier to write.

A Straightforward Vocabulary

Your readers will appreciate your writing more if you say what you mean directly and concisely. They can read faster because it takes less work to comprehend what you are saying and your work may simply be shorter than if you use a lot of flowery language or ponderous phrases. For example, you don't need to "make an adjustment to" the bed, you need to "adjust the bed." You don't need to be "in agreement with" your neighbor over who shoveled snow the last time, you just need to agree.

You want to avoid jargon and clichés. We see these expressions, but it helps to define them.

Jargon is specialized or technical language. It may be appropriate to fill an internal company memo with it, since all the readers will be familiar with the terminology. Generally, you want to stay away from this "in-the-know" language, as it makes your readers feel left out if they are not accustomed to it.

Clichés are overused or pat phrases, such as "nervous as a cat in a room full of rocking chairs" or "neat as a pin." For most of your writing, it is better to say someone is nervous or describe that a room or desk looks neat. If you are writing fiction, you may create a character whose speech is full of clichés. For most nonfiction writing, you want to avoid clichés like the plague (so to speak).

A DIRECT WRITING STYLE

Some people like to take long country drives, unworried about their destination. Most of the rest of the people on the planet have places to go and things to do. Your writing is for them. They haven't got all day, and your writing should value their time.

Roundabout writing: Good retirement planning should have the specific goals of letting you live your life independently and making it possible for you not to have to rely on your children for financial support.

Clear Writing: Good retirement planning enables you to live independently, without relying on your children for financial support.

Roundabout writing: It is hoped that the Community Bazaar Planning Committee can come together at least a couple of times every month so that the problems associated with last year's stampede on the funnel cake stand can be avoided.

Clear Writing: I hope the Community Bazaar Planning Committee will meet at least twice a month, so they can develop ways to avoid problems such as last year's stampede on the funnel cake stand.

Why You Should Care About Active Voice

In a sentence written in active voice, the subject of the sentence is the "doer of the action," while in passive voice sentences the subject is the receiver.

Passive voice: The dog was hit by the car.

Active voice: The car hit the dog.

In this case, the reader can still get the point. However, passive voice can make it difficult to understand a writer's point. The "doer" of the action may even be missing from a sentence.

Passive voice: Each recipe should be written so that they can be understood by the reviewers.

Active voice: Each cook should write their recipes so the reviewers can understand them. (You might be able to guess that a cook would write the recipe, but it could be someone else.)

Passive voice: Consideration will be given to your idea and a memo will be sent to you to say what management did with your suggestion.

Active voice: The ABC branch will consider your idea and the branch supervisor will let you know whether the company will act on your suggestion. (In this case, passive voice obscured information about who would consider the idea and who would get back to the person who made the suggestion. If readers get to the end of one of your sentences and cannot tell who did what to whom, they have a problem. And so do you.)

Sometimes passive voice is a deliberate choice. A good example in film is in *Star Trek VI, the Undiscovered Country*. The Klingon prosecutor asks Captain Kirk if he said something particularly incriminating. Kirk hesitates a moment and then says, "Those words were spoken by me." He sure wanted to take the emphasis off himself. In bureaucracies, such wording could be called a "CYA" presentation of the facts. (So much for avoiding jargon.)

GRAMMAR GRUMBLERS

There are entire books that teach you how to apply the English language's many rules of grammar. It is good to have one as a reference, but it does not have to be a fancy one, or even one that is brand new. Pick up one at a used book sale. This section gives some very basic information on common grammar problems and how to spot them.

Subject verb agreement

The closer the verb is to the noun, the easier it is for you to make sure you have a singular noun with a singular verb, and a plural noun with a plural verb. Sometimes there is information between the subject and verb that adds some confusion. For example:

The kingdom, replete with valleys and streams, has a large deposit of iron ore. The word "kingdom" is the subject, so even though the plural word "streams" comes just before the verb, the verb must agree with the singular subject.

Patrick and Jennifer go to the state fair every year. (plural verb)

Susan or Anthony has the key. (singular verb)

The first sentence requires a plural verb because the conjunction is "and." When the two subjects are joined by "or," the sentence requires a singular verb.

Confusion Between Possessive Case and Contractions

If you have trouble with contractions, you are not alone. The best way to keep straight is to remember that the word with the apostrophe is really two words. You may have to read a sentence aloud, substituting both words, to check which is correct.

Many contraction problems are because the contraction gets mixed up with the possessive. Think of the possessive case as a pronoun that claims ownership. Here are some examples.

- It's really hard for a dog to remember where it buried its bones.

Its (without the apostrophe) is always possessive. If you substituted "it is" before bones, the sentence would not make any sense, so leave it at its.

- Your mother wondered when you're coming home.

"Your" (no apostrophe) is possessive and "you're" substitutes for "you are."

- They're going there after the play, with their parents.

A lot of writers have trouble with their, there, and they're. As you can tell from the context of the sentence, "their" is possessive" and "they're" is the shortened version of "they are." "There" refers to a place or location.

Parallel structure

Parallel structure comes into play when you have lists of phrases. If one is a full sentence, they all need to be. If one starts with a noun, they all need to start with a noun.

Each parent makes a choice to:

Non-parallel structure
- Teach their children about drugs.
- Ignoring warning signs of drug use
- Carefully watch their children's friends

Parallel structure
- Teach their children about drugs
- Ignore warning signs of drug use
- Watch their children's friends carefully

A reader can understand each phrase when you use non-parallel structure, but the material is easier to read when the basic structure of the phrase (in this case, verb/noun) is the same. Parallel structure is about balance.

Where to put modifiers

Misplaced and so-called dangling modifiers give editors plenty to chuckle about. Essentially, these words or phrases are placed in a sentence such that it is hard to tell what they modify.

- I saw a woman running through the supermarket with one shoe.
- I saw a woman with one shoe running through the supermarket.

The second sentence clarifies it is the woman who was minus a shoe, not the supermarket.

- The teacher said Friday the exams would be finished.
- On Friday, the teacher said the exams would be finished.
- The teacher said the exams would be finished on Friday.

The final sentence clarifies whether the teacher spoke on Friday or referred to what would happen on Friday.

- Never having played tennis, good athletic shoes don't concern Jeff.
- Never having played tennis, Jeff is not concerned about good athletic shoes.

It is Jeff who never played tennis, not the shoes.

Punctuation Makes a Difference

Period or question mark? No problem. Comma or semicolon? Ummmm.

Punctuation should mirror our speech patterns. If we would pause slightly, a comma could be appropriate. If we come to something close to a full top, it's more likely to be a semicolon.

A few examples of when to use a comma:
- Between words in a list of words
- Between the date and the year (February 14, 1995)

- To separate a lead-in phrase from the rest of a sentence (Although it was past midnight, Mark kept studying for the exam.)
- To enclose a phrase within a sentence (The Jones family farmhouse, old though it was, won the contest for best home design.)
- To set off the word however. (It is unwise, however, to wait until July to plant seeds.)

When not to use a comma:
- Between the month and year. (It should be February 1995 – no comma needed.)
- When it would interrupt the flow of a thought. (At the edge of the cliff, stood a warning sign.) This comma is unnecessary and should be removed.

Semicolons are used to separate phrases, or to separate two distinct parts of a sentence.
- Among the things a new teacher has to consider are: whether to stand or sit when giving lectures; how to greet students on the first day of school; and how much time to devote to grading papers each evening.
- Thomas was the best cook in the family; his sister Sarah was a better snow shoveler.

The colon's primary use is to direct a reader's attention to a list, as in the preceding example of the new teacher. It has become fashionable among some writers to leave it out, and just start the list. It's not clear who thought of this idea; it can make the sentences harder to read. Before you know it, you're in the middle of a list, and you don't know when it started.

Hyphens: the Problem Children

Hyphens link two words that can be used separately, but when used together (as an adjective) should be linked.
- Local residents know Angela's bookstore very well.
- Angela's bookstore is well-known to local residents.

Think of the two words as modifiers joining force. Other examples are:
- high-fashion neighborhood
- spine-tingling thriller
- eighteenth-century house
- much-loved teacher

Hyphens are not used when the first adjective ends in "ly."
- highly qualified teacher
- newly minted coin

Hyphens are also used for a range of compound expressions, such as sister-in-law. Many words that used to use hyphens have now become one word – non-profit is now nonprofit, for example.

Dual Punctuation

The most important thing to remember is that if you are writing in the United States, the period and comma always go inside (before) the closing quotation marks. The semicolon and colon go outside (after) the closing quotation marks. It's different in England; don't worry about it.

- The title of the book was "Catch 22."
- "A stitch in time saves nine," my grandmother always said.
- Titles of individuals can be lower-cased, as with "president of the United States;" unless they precede someone's name, as in President George Washington.
- The teacher began with the classic "Winnie-the-Pooh," first describing Pooh's magnificent house in the tree trunk.

It's even more complicated for question marks and exclamation points. They go inside the closing quotation marks if the punctuation was part of the original quotation; otherwise, they go outside.

- She asked, "Did you get home on time?"
- Did you answer, "Yes, I did"?

Don't let yourself **even think** about things such as dual punctuation marks as you write your first and second draft. These are final-polish items.

A Few Words on Respectful Language

For centuries, the English language used the term "man" to include all humanity. As more women have moved into the workforce, it has become customary to distinguish between men and women when a statement includes both. This makes language more precise and enables women and girls to feel included in a speaker's or writer's audience.

Gender-specific terms such as "manpower" have evolved to workforce or personnel. The National Aeronautics and Space Administration (NASA) has officially abandoned the term "manned space flight," referring instead to "crewed missions" or other inclusive terminology. Still sometimes used are terms such as "manmade lake" or "man-hours" of work. There are substitutes, such as "staff-hours," or it may be a case of reworking a sentence. You can say, for example, a "human-built lake," or rephrase to talk about a "lake local engineers built."

Are we talking about another form of political correctness here? No. The impact of the words we use and the images we convey are far more important. Not all biased terminology has the word "man" in it. Phrases such as "old wives' tale" impart the idea that an anecdote relayed by a woman is frivolous or not to be believed. The message this conveys is stored by children--boys and girls--forming impressions about their roles in the world and the value of one another's opinions.

Some phrases slight the role of men in society. A discussion of "motherly instincts" in child rearing implies that fathers are less nurturing parents than mothers. Other expressions highlight men as the bad guys. In talking about parents who do not pay child support, the phrase deadbeat dad has become popular. While men are more likely to pay child support than women, it is not fair to single them out as the only sex that does not make these payments.

As important as gender-neutral language is language that treats all ethnic and racial groups respectfully. Surely you would not deliberately write to offend, but there may be expressions you use that are not appropriate. Preferences do evolve, and are not always in sync. For example, some individuals prefer the term Hispanic, others prefer Latino. Here again, you are back to your audience.

Pronouns are often at the root of problems. Even the use of "they" can be disrespectful if the writer uses it to imply that "they" have a problem and "they" is a certain group of workers or race of employees.

Some ways to avoid male and female pronouns (other than when you are specifically referring to men and women) are:

Use a plural word. In general, make sure the rest of your sentence follows the same usage pattern.

- The average American drives his car 40 miles per day could become:
  On average, Americans drive their cars 40 miles per day.

- Use "they" or "their" as if they were singular.
  Anyone who swims in the motel pool after 5 p.m. does so at their own risk.
  "I shouldn't like to punish anyone, even if they'd done me wrong." That's a quote from
  George Eliot, who died in 1880. By the way, George was a woman – author Mary Ann
  Evans, who did not think she could publish with a woman's name. Times do change.

Much More to Discuss

As you can see, a reference book will be very handy. This chapter could be a 300-page book. (Look, another use for a hyphen!) It is hard to know when to look something up if you don't think the way you do it is a problem. It may make sense to page through a book that covers grammar and style as you watch your next football game or ice skating championship. That will help you get a better sense of when you might have a problem.

Get a fairly simple book. You don't need to know every option for correct grammar and usage. You only need enough to make your point.

CHAPTER FIVE
TAKING THE FEAR
OUT OF REVISING YOUR WORK

When you begin to reread your work, preferably a day or at least a few hours after you've written it, pretend you are what is called a "cold reader;" someone who was not involved in writing the piece. This will give you the perspective of someone with less familiarity, and it may make you more willing to make changes.

Don't worry if you don't like what you see. If you keep an open mind, you'll be able to make changes. If you beat yourself up about what a "bad" writer you are, your emotions will get in the way of clear thinking.

Read your draft with pencil in hand. Make some notes in the margin, or circle spelling and punctuation errors. You don't want to get too bogged down with detailed corrections at this point; just get a sense of the overall piece and how it flows.

Some broad questions to ask as you consider your first draft:

- Who will read this, and are the vocabulary and tone of the piece appropriate for these readers?
- What was the purpose of writing this, and does the piece achieve that purpose?
- Is all of the material relevant to the purpose, or does the writing wander into areas that do not need to be there for the reader to get the point?
- Does the ending segment clearly draw a close to the piece? Does it present the conclusions, summarize key points, or otherwise offer some closure?

If you don't think the piece fulfilled its purpose, make some notes or talk aloud about what is missing or whether the information is "buried" in the piece rather than stated clearly. If you've written a relatively short piece, you might want to read all of it aloud, or ask someone to read it to you.

STARTING THE REVISIONS

Take it one paragraph or group of paragraphs at a time. If a cliché will help, remember that Rome wasn't built in a day. Although it is fine to make corrections to individual sentences, if you find yourself scribbling all over a paragraph, put it aside and start it from scratch. You may find that the paragraph rewrite goes faster than a struggle over individual words or sentence order.

As you revise, look at some more specific aspects of your piece.

- Do you make some points more than once? If you see phrases such as, "As stated previously.." you should decide the best place to put the point, and say it once. Even if you don't have such phrases, be sure you don't repeat yourself.
- Is the information you present specific enough to support the conclusion you reached at the end of the piece? Alternatively, is there so much detail about the supporting information that your reader's head may be spinning?
- Is the tone of your paper the same throughout? If you write informally in some places and formally in others, pick one style and stick with it.
- Have you written largely in active voice (where the subject of the sentence is the doer of the action)?

Whether you are making major or minor revisions, the word processor is your best friend. You can block and move sentences or paragraphs, check your spelling, and even get word substitutes if you see you use one word too often. The only danger to the word processing software is that the printed copy looks so neat you hate to change it. Wrong! Tear it apart.

Some Specific Nits to Look For

- Have you used any redundant word patterns, such as future plans, important essentials, or specific details? If so, pick one and ditch the other.
- Do you have some very long sentences? If you have sentences of more than twenty words, consider breaking them into two sentences. Twenty is not a magic number; look for places where there are many points in one sentence.
- Are you using phrases when you could use single words? For example, "at this point in time" means "now."
- Do you have lots of sentences ending in prepositions? Some are okay, but if you see dozens, make a few changes. You don't need to go overboard. Winston Churchill once said, "Ending a sentence with a preposition is something up with which I will not put." That's going overboard.

Some people say that every draft goes immediately into revision mode. It is tempting to say revise until you are happy with the piece, but if you are new to clear writing, that may be too much to ask of yourself. Writing is a learned process, and you don't learn algebra in one week, so why writing? As they say in twelve step programs, it's progress, not perfection.

CHAPTER SIX
WHERE DO YOU GO FROM HERE?

The more you write, the better you get. Keep writing about things you know and like, and you will be able to see your progress more clearly than if you only write at work.

Most community colleges have courses in writing, and a number of universities have correspondence programs. You can learn a lot in a correspondence program, and the structure of having to complete projects is good discipline. However, the interactions within a classroom can be more fun. If you are not sure what courses are available in your area, call the English Department in a nearby community college or university, or ask at a bookstore.

If you visit any bookstore or web sites such as Amazon.com, you will find dozens of books on writing. Listed below are some good text resources. With today's ease of publishing, you will find many other options.

Starting from Scratch: a Different Kind of Writers' Manual, Rita Mae Brown, Bantam Books, NY, 1989.

Thinking on Paper: Refine, Express, and Actually Generate Ideas by Understanding the Processes of the Mind, V.A. Howard and J.H Barton, Quill, NY, 1986.

The Scott, Foresman Handbook for Writers, Maxine Hairston and John J. Ruszkiewicz, Now published by Longman, formerly by Harper Collins, NY. Newer editions have more authors and are very expensive. An older one will do.

Writing to Learn, William Zinsser, Harper and Row, NY, 1989.

Grammar for Grownups: a Guide to Grammar and Usage for Everyone Who has to Put Words on Paper Effectively, Val Dumond, Harper Collins, NY, 1993.

This is a neat website, with a simple cover page and concise definitions. It is written by a UK organization, so there might be subtle differences from American English, but I don't see them. http://www.edufind.com/english-grammar/english-grammar-guide/

There are a number of websites that discuss grammar and give writing tips. One site (Legal Productivity) has links to ten sites. It's a long website name, but worth noting.

http://www.legalproductivity.com/practice-management/top-10-grammar-websites-for-bloggers-and-writers/

While you can learn a lot from books, classes, and website, writing is a lot like swimming. You just have to get into pool or you'll never do it well.

The more aware you are of how others write, the more you improve your own writing. How do you do this? Read. You'll find yourself admiring how much a good writer can pack into a sentence, or how well an author describes a complex situation.

Keep writing, and remember, even the best writers question their ability on any given day.

There is no security, no assurance that because we wrote something good two months ago, we will do it again. Actually, every time we begin, we wonder how we ever did it before.
Natalie Goldberg, *Writing Down the Bones*

AUTHOR BIO

Elaine L. Orr is a native Washingtonian who relocated to Iowa in the mid-1990s. She worked as a technical writer and writing consultant, and did analytical work in the U.S. and overseas. She also writes novels, plays and poetry, and her play *Permission to Hope* was given a staged reading by The Writer's Center of Bethesda, Maryland. Her pictorial history of Monett, MO is part of Arcadia Publishing's Images of America series. A number of Elaine's novels are available at on-line booksellers, in audio, ebook, and paper formats. Among these are the Jolie Gentil cozy mystery series. She likes to put children in her stories, probably the result of enjoying time spent with her four siblings and their families. She lives with her husband, Jim Larkin and her cats, both of whom like to inspect the keyboard as she works.

elaineorr55@yahoo.com
www.elaineorr.com
www.elaineorr.blogspot.com

If you would like to see how I use these techniques in fiction and other nonfiction, here are some options. Many are in audio. Paperbacks can be ordered on line or through a book store or library. Support your independent booksellers!

The Jolie Gentil Cozy Mystery Series
Real estate appraiser, Jolie Gentil has a schedule flexible enough to get in trouble in her Jersey shore town. The series has been termed "fiction you can share with your mom" and "mysteries minus the yuck factor." They're not boring, but you won't find detailed autopsy reports and such.

Appraisal for Murder
Rekindling Motives
When the Carny Comes to Town
Any Port in a Storm
Trouble on the Doorstep
Behind the Walls
Vague Images
Ground to a Halt
Jolie and Scoobie High School Misadventures (prequel)
Also look for boxed sets of the Jolie books, on various websites. These are not in paperback.

Other Fiction
At all sites
Secrets of the Gap – ancient and modern mysteries in England's Roman Baths.
Searching for Secrets – an Iowa City teacher and police officer try to stop drug dealers.
Biding Time – coming-of-age story of a Vietnam Vet's nephew. Geared to young adults.
Selected Nonfiction
500+ Hashtags for Writers – reference tools for authors who use Twitter.
Monett – part of Arcadia Publishing's Images of America Series

THE INITIAL IDEA LIST

These are numbered so you can distinguish between items, but your initial idea list is a free-flowing batch of thoughts, in no particular order. (You may photocopy this page.)

1.

2.

3.

4.

5.

6.

7.

8.

9.

10.

11.

12.

13.

14.

REFINED IDEA LIST

Now you're organizing those thoughts. Think of broad themes
and group together those ideas that deal with similar subjects.
(You may photocopy this page.)

_____

1.

2.

3.

4.

5.

_____

1.

2.

3.

4.

5.

_____

1.

2.

3.

4.

5.

_____

1.

2.

3.

4.

5.

_____

1.

2.

3.

4.

5.

_____

1.

2.

3.

4.

5.

www.ingramcontent.com/pod-product-compliance
Lightning Source LLC
Chambersburg PA
CBHW081157280526
45787CB00008B/3367